THE WHOLE STORY OF CHRISTMAS

EVERYTHING THE BIBLE TELLS US ABOUT THE NATIVITY OF JESUS CHRIST

Written and Compiled by:
HUGH & KAYE MARTIN

Presented by:
[YOUR CHURCH, DENOMINATION, OR ORGANIZATION HERE]

AK Publishing
P.O. Box 1736, Sebastopol, CA 95473
AKLearning@Gmail.com

Library of Congress Cataloging-in-Publication data

THE WHOLE STORY OF CHRISTMAS: Everything the Bible Tells Us about the Nativity of Jesus Christ
/Hugh Martin and Amalia Kaye Martin
Cover design, book design, & graphics: Hugh Martin

COLOR, BLACK-ON-WHITE EDITION 5. King James/Good News, Church Imprint version. CBW5 – KJ/GN/CI
Printed in the United States of America
ISBN: 9798344758886
Non-fiction, Religion (Holidays, Christmas and Advent)

HUGH MARTIN is listed in Who's Who in the United States and Who's Who in the World. Mr. Martin received his degrees and credentials from Swarthmore College, University of Pennsylvania, Indiana University, and University of California, Berkeley. Hugh has appeared on numerous talk shows, led seminars at many colleges and corporations, and spoken at numerous professional conferences. Mr. Martin is past president of the investment brokerage and advisory firm, Hugh Martin Securities. Hugh Martin has had a lifelong interest in the Bible and its impact on Western Civilization – an influence that he studied in detail during his Master's and Doctoral work in English and Comparative Literature. In keeping with Mr. Martin's field of expertise, this book is intended as a literary interpretation of the Bible, not a theological one. Controversial issues – such as the historical veracity of the Bible, the Divinity of Christ, the events of the End Times, and the role of the Jews in Christ's execution – are beyond the scope of this book.

AMALIA KAYE MARTIN ('Kaye') received her degrees and certifications from California State Fullerton and Baumann College. Kaye has been an early-education specialist in the Sonoma County Public Schools, a community activist, and a member of the Occidental, CA Community Council. She has been a home-school coordinator and an instructor in nutrition and natural medicine at Baumann College. Hugh and Kaye have five multi-gifted children, all with strong family ties.

[Example of a Church Imprint:] **Victory OUTREACH INTERNATIONAL** is a church that brings together believers from many races, ethnicities, and nations – Hispanics, Afro-Americans, Native Americans, Asian Americans, Africans, Polynesians, and peoples of European descent. The Church's 700+ branches and ministries in America and in 30 foreign countries are renowned for their life-changing, year-long, no-cost Recovery Homes – where former drug addicts, alcoholics, gang members, and ex-convicts are transformed by the healing power of Jesus Christ – then set on a path to a new and brighter future.

CUSTOMIZED VERSIONS OF THIS BOOK. This book is available at cost to churches, ministries, social improvement organizations, and individuals with a heart for the Lord's Word. When ordering in quantity, you may substitute your organization's own name and location, along with a write-up of your own organization on this page. Customized versions may also include your own preferred translations of Bible passages and any changes in the explanatory text you think appropriate. The cost for a full-color, oversize book like this one is normally less than $10 per book. Please contact the authors for further details: AKLearning@Gmail.com.

WHY THE KING JAMES? The King James version of the Bible was translated in the time of Shakespeare and written in the language of Shakespeare. It is also one of the versions that is most faithful to the original text. In the authors' opinion, the King James is the only Bible in English that is great literature – with great language, great characterizations, great symbolic resonance, and the greatest evocation of spiritual Truth. In other words, the King James can be viewed as a divinely-inspired translation – just as its source is viewed as a divinely-inspired original.

COVER & INTERIOR ILLUSTRATIONS. In the same spirit as the King James, the illustrations in this book show how the greatest visionaries of Western Civilization viewed these remarkable characters and their amazing stories. Cover and Frontispiece 1: *Madonna of the Magnificat* , by Sandro Botticelli. Frontispiece 2: *Virgin and Child with Saint Anne*, by Leonardo Da Vinci. Frontispiece 3: *Adoration of the Shepherds*, by Domenico Ghirlandaio. Thanks are also given for permissions to use images throughout this book. Some permissions pending.

THE WHOLE STORY OF CHRISTMAS

EVERYTHING THE BIBLE TELLS US ABOUT THE NATIVITY OF JESUS Christ

Written and Compiled by:
HUGH & KAYE MARTIN

Presented by:
[YOUR CHURCH, DENOMINATION, OR ORGANIZATION HERE]

AK PUBLISHING
Sebastopol, CA
2024

TABLE OF CONTENTS

Section C. *After the Birth of Christ*

Episode 11. Presentation at the Temple (p. 35)

When Joseph and Mary bring the Baby Jesus to the temple in Jerusalem for the ritual sacrifice, there appears an old man named Simeon – who identifies Jesus as the Promised Messiah and rejoices that he has lived to see this day.

Episode 12. Visit by the Wise Men (p. 37)

Three Wise Men appear in Jerusalem– inquiring of King Herod after the promised King of the Jews, whose star they have seen in the East. Guided on by that same star, they find the Holy Family in Bethlehem, where they worship Jesus and present three special gifts.

Episode 13. Flight into Egypt (p. 39)

Warned in a dream that King Herod has evil intentions, the Holy Family escapes by night, and flees into the land of Egypt.

Episode 14. Slaughter of the Innocents (p. 41)

Fearing that the prophesied King of the Jews represents a threat to his rule, King Herod orders every young child born near Bethlehem to be slaughtered.

Episode 15. Return to Nazareth (p. 43)

Once they hear that King Herod is dead, the Holy Family returns to Israel – but then is diverted to the town of Nazareth in Galilee, because they fear the wrath of Herod's son, Archelaus.

Episode 16. Fulfillment of the Prophecies (p. 45)

The prophesies made during Jesus's lifetime are fulfilled by the spread of Christianity to the far ends of the Earth, and by Jesus's eternal reign at the right hand of God.

Introduction:
The Whole Story of Christmas

What is the Story of Christmas? Is it Jolly Old Saint Nick – who 'shakes when he laughs like a bowl full of jelly?' Is it Rudolf the Red-Nosed Reindeer—whose shiny nose leads Santa's sleigh through that foggy Christmas night? Is it Frosty the Snowman – who comes to life when the children place that old silk hat on his head? Is it even White Christmas – where Bing Crosby and Rosemary Clooney put on a musical extravaganza to save their Vermont country inn from financial ruin?

No, you say. It's the story of Jesus Christ and his birth. But even there, we must ask: Is the Christmas Story just the Angel appearing to Mary? And Joseph and Mary's journey to Bethlehem – where they must sleep in a stable, because there's no room at the inn? And the scene by the Manger – where the Shepherds from the hillside gather to worship the sleeping Babe? And even the three Wise Men – following 'yonder star' until they arrive at the stable to join the Shepherds in worship of the Babe? Well yes, that is part of the Story of Christmas, but not the Whole Story – and not even an entirely accurate story.

The Whole Story of Christmas. According to the Gospels, the Whole Story of Christmas occurs in fourteen distinct episodes: Beginning about 15 months before the Birth of Christ -- with conception of Christ's precursor, John the Baptist. And ending perhaps four years after the Birth – with the return of Joseph and Mary from Egypt, where they had fled to escape the wrath of King Herod.

Celebrating the Advent of Christmas. In olden times, everyone knew the Whole Story of Christmas, because each of the 14 episodes of Christ's Birth was celebrated and dramatized in stories, in plays, in pageants, in rituals and ceremonies, in songs, in pictures, in feasts and festivals – with the fourteen events spread in a continuing stream over the last four weeks (or even the whole Fall season) leading up to Christmas Day. All together, this series of events was known as the Celebration of the Advent.

How this Book Celebrates the Advent. This book is an effort to revive, invigorate, and amplify the Celebration of the Advent. It does so by focusing attention in turn on each of the fourteen episodes of Christ's Birth – framing them with two more episodes: At the beginning, the Prophecies that foretold the Coming of Christ the Messiah. At the end, the Fulfillment of those Prophesies – passages that proclaim how this Coming of Christ has transformed the world.

Layout of this Book. Each two-page spread of Main Section of this book focuses on a single episode of Christ's Birth. On the right side is the full text of that episode from the King James Bible. Below that, or to the left, is the same episode in modern language, as translated by the Good News Bible. Below the name of that episode is a brief explanation of what occurred, and why that episode is significant. Accompanying these written words is a selection of great classic and contemporary art depicting that event – with captions drawn from those sections of Scripture.

In the full book, the Main Section is followed by two additional sections – resources to help you in your own Celebration of the Advent: First, a selection of **songs and carols** from around the world that show how various nations and cultures celebrate Christ's Birth. Second, a selection of **movies and miniseries**, that either a) Depict the various events of Christ's Birth, or b) Tell some more contemporary story that conveys the true meaning of Christmas.

Your Celebrations of the Advent. Here are some of the ways this book can help with your own Celebration of the Advent:

- **Personal Study and Contemplation.** Beginning in early Fall, set aside time each week to study and contemplate one or two of the episodes of the Christmas Story. Are you studying frequently enough to cover the entire Christmas Story by the time Christmas arrives? Do the episodes have greater meaning for you, now that they are tied in to the Whole Story?
- **Bible Readings.** Read the section from your favorite Bible version that describes that episode. Are you reading these familiar selections by rote – or do you really understand and appreciate what you're reading? Can you decipher the difficult or archaic words and phrases? Do you detect a symbolic as well as a literal meaning? Do you continue to gain insights from the passage each time you read it?
- **Songs and Carols.** Along with your readings, sing (with your family or study group) songs and carols from the full book appropriate to the season – and, where possible, appropriate to

the episode you are studying. For carols that are familiar favorites, what do the lyrics actually mean? Does the music fill you with an exhilaration that goes beyond what mere words evoke?

- **The Story in Pictures.** As you study each episode, look carefully at the great art that accompanies the Bible verses. What aspect of the event does the artist focus on? How does the artist's interpretation differ from your own imagining of the event? How does the picture enhance your understanding and appreciation of that event?
- **The Story in Movies.** Watch a variety of the Christmas movies and mini-series described in the movie section of the full book.

  When you watch movies that depict the actual Christmas Story, ask yourself: What episodes does the movie concentrate on – and which ones are minimized or left out? Who are the most vivid and memorable characters – and what are their main positive and negative qualities?

  When you watch more contemporary Christmas movies, what is the meaning of Christmas that they are conveying? Which characters are most vivid and memorable? Is there some part of the meaning of Christmas that enlightens or transforms them? Are there other Christmas movies that distort or denigrate the meaning of Christmas?
- **The Christmas Pageant.** If you belong to a church or community group, organize or participate in a Christmas Pageant – preferably one that faithfully portrays the Whole Story of Christmas. Will this be a typical corner-church Christmas Pageant – or can you add appealing dramatic and musical elements that will draw in visitors from the surrounding community, and beyond? How can you engage many members of your church in the production – so they become participants as well as spectators?
- **The Christmas Choral Concert.** At that same church or community group, organize or participate in a Christmas Choral Concert – preferably one that is faithful to the true Story of Christmas. Include songs from various nations and cultures, as found in the music section of this book. Does the music you are presenting match the audience you are singing to? Are you showing your audience new and original ways to celebrate the season? Is the audience invited to join in the singing?
- **The Christmas Sermons.** If you are in a position to do so, preach a series of messages from the pulpit of your church that focus on the various episodes of the Christmas Story. How can you use those episodes to build your congregation's faith, their knowledge of the Savior they worship, and their commitment to the goals of your church?
- **The Musical Worship.** Accompany each message from the pulpit with Christmas music by the choir and congregation that reinforces and enhances that message. Are you giving your congregation a mixture of familiar, comfortable old favorites – along with new songs that stimulate new ways of thinking about the Christmas Season?
- **Christmas Study Groups.** In your church or community study group, focus discussion on the same episode of the Christmas Story that is featured in that week's Sermon and Musical Worship. How does the particular episode speak to your own life situation – and to the situations of other members of the group?
- **Missions Work.** All the elements of a Christmas Program for your local church can be even more effective in communicating with other cultures -- cultures that speak other languages, as well as cultures that communicate more by images and actions than by words. With ethnic cultures, for example, a Pageant that <u>shows</u> the Birth of Christ can be more effective than a Bible verse that just <u>tells</u> of that same Birth.
- **The Transforming Power of Christ.** After the Christmas Season is over, continue to focus your awareness on the Christmas Story and on the Meaning of Christmas. Is the Christmas Story just a feel-good experience, before the harsh reality of the New Year sets in? Can the Christmas Season bring about a change of heart that you can carry through the entire following year? Are you allowing the Power of Christ to transform you permanently to the very core of your being?

A CONFLUENCE OF MIRACLES:
SUPERNATURAL OCCURRENCES DURING THE ADVENT OF JESUS CHRIST

FORTY-EIGHT MIRACULOUS EVENTS. The story of the Advent of Jesus Christ contains the highest concentration of supernatural occurrences to be found anywhere in the Bible. All told, there are fifteen supernatural **Visitations**, three outright **Miracles**, five **Signs** verifying future events, three highly unlikely **Coincidences**, four **instances of Extra Sensory Perception** (ESP), seven fulfillments of **Past Prophesies**, and eleven present pronouncements of **Future Prophesies** that come true – often with corroboration by multiple **Witnesses**.

WHY THESE EVENTS ARE IMPORTANT. This great Confluence of Miracles is not just an interesting story. It indicates that a great move of God took place with the birth of Jesus Christ. In fact, it is evidence that **the Advent of Jesus Christ (along with Easter) is the most important event recorded in the Bible**. There is further evidence: Although the Life of Christ concentrates primarily on just the three years of Christ's Ministry, it comprises almost one-tenth of the entire 3000-year span of Bible. And although the events of Christmas and Easter take place primarily in just a few days, these two events comprise over one-third of the entire Life of Christ. This centrality of the Life of Christ also has further implications: The entire Old Testament is just a foreshadowing of Christ. All of the Bible after Christ is just a working-out of the reverberations of Christ's brief presence.

Furthermore, if we view the events of Christ's life to be literally true, then the Life of Christ is not just a pretty story. It is factual history. And if the Life of Christ is history, then **the Advent of Jesus Christ is the greatest event ever to take place in human history**. All events that occurred before Christ are just a foreshadowing and preparation for Christ's Coming. All events of history that have occurred since Christ are just a working-out of the implications of Christ's influence. Thus, even the smallest details of the Advent of Jesus Christ are of supreme importance.

To show you just how extraordinary these events are, here are all **forty-eight supernatural occurrences**, in the order of their appearance:

Episode 2. Annunciation of John to Zacharias

- **Visitation 1.** The old priest Zacharias is visited by the Angel Gabriel in the Temple.
- **Miracle 1.** Zacharias and his ancient and barren wife Elizabeth conceive a baby. (see Episode 6)
- **Sign 1.** Zacharias is struck dumb by Angel Gabriel – a Sign that Gabriel's prediction will come true. (see Episode 6)
- **Past Prophesy 1.** The coming of John the Baptist was prophesied 600 years before by the Prophet Isaiah.
- **Future Prophesy 1.** John the Baptist will prepare the way for the coming of Jesus Christ. (see Episode 6)
- **Sign 2.** The unborn Baby John will be filled with the Holy Spirit when he first encounters the unborn Baby Jesus. (see Episode 4)

Episode 3. Annunciation to Mary

- **Visitation 2.** The Virgin Mary is visited by the Angel Gabriel.
- **Miracle 2.** While yet a Virgin, Mary is to conceive a child. (see Episode 4)
- **Sign 3.** When Mary meets her old and barren cousin Elizabeth, Mary will find her to be already six-months' pregnant. (see Episode 4)
- **Future Prophesy 2.** Mary predicts that her baby Jesus Christ will become known as the Son of God.

Visitation 2. The Angel Gabriel appears to Mary -- announcing her Virgin Birth.

Episode 4. Mary Visits Elizabeth

- **Sign 3** (fulfilled). When Mary meets her old and barren cousin Elizabeth, she finds her to be in fact six-months' pregnant. (see Episode 3)
- **ESP 1.** When they first meet, Elizabeth knows Mary is pregnant, even though Mary is too early to show.
- **Visitation 3.** Elizabeth is filled with the Holy Spirit, and bursts forth in a song of ecstatic praise.
- **Sign 2** (fulfilled). Upon first encountering the unborn Baby Jesus, the unborn Baby John leaps for joy in Elizabeth's womb. (see Episode 2)
- **ESP 2.** Elizabeth knows that, from the very beginning, Mary believed the Angel Gabriel and submitted to God's Will – unlike Zacharias. (see Episodes 2 and 3)

Episode 5. The Song of Mary

- **Visitation 4.** Mary is filled with the Holy Spirit, and bursts forth in a song of ecstatic praise for God's power and mercy.
- **Future Prophesy 3.** Mary predicts that all future generations will bless and revere her.

Episode 6. The Birth of John

- **Miracle 1** (fulfilled). The old and barren Elizabeth does in fact give birth. (see Episode 2)
- **Sign 1** (completed). Zacharias's speech of restored, once he fully believes the Angel Gabriel's prophesy. (see Episode 2)
- **Visitation 5.** Zacharias is filled with the Holy Spirit, and bursts forth in a song of ecstatic praise.
- **Future Prophesy 4.** Zacharias predicts that Jesus Christ will become the world's Redeemer.
- **Future Prophesy 5.** Zacharias predicts that his boy John will prepare the way for Jesus Christ.

Episode 7. Annunciation to Joseph

- **Visitation 6.** Joseph is visited in a dream by the Holy Spirit.
- **ESP 3.** Joseph knows by the Holy Spirit that Mary has not had relations with any other man, and that her baby was conceived by the Holy Spirit. (see Episode 3)
- **Past Prophesy 2.** Joseph recognizes that Mary's virgin birth was foretold by the Prophet Isaiah over 600 years before.

Episode 8. Journey to Bethlehem

- **Coincidence 1.** The decree by Roman Emperor Augustus requires Joseph to return to the ancestral birthplace of King David, Bethlehem.
- **Past Prophesy 3.** Over 700 years before, the Prophet Micah predicted that the Promised Messiah would come from Bethlehem.

Episode 9. Annunciation to the Shepherds

- **Visitation 7.** An Angel appears to Shepherds in the fields outside of Bethlehem.
- **Past Prophesy 3** (fulfilled). As announced by the Angel, the Promised Messiah is indeed born in Bethlehem. (see Episode 8)
- **Sign 4.** As a Sign that the Angel's assertion is true, the Angel predicts the Shepherds will find the Baby Jesus wrapped in swaddling clothes, and lying in the most unlikely of cradles, a manger. (see Episode 10)
- **Visitation 8.** A whole army of Angels appears to the Shepherds, praising God for this glorious event.

Visitation 7. An Angel appears to Shepherds in the fields near Bethlehem.

MIRACLES SURROUNDING THE ADVENT OF JESUS CHRIST (cont.)

Episode 10. Nativity of Jesus

- **Sign 4** (fulfilled)**.** The Shepherds do in fact find the Baby Jesus in a humble stable -- wrapped in swaddling clothes and lying in a manger. (see Episode 9)

Episode 11. Presentation at the Temple

- **Visitation 9.** The devout old man Simeon has previously been visited by the Holy Spirit, who predicted that he would live to see the Coming Messiah.
- **Visitation 10.** As the Holy Family arrives at the Temple, the Holy Spirit visits Simeon again – revealing to him that the Messiah has now come to the Temple.
- **Coincidence 2.** At the very moment the Holy Family enters the Temple, Simeon appears there to greet them.
- **Visitation 11.** Simeon is filled with the Holy Spirit and bursts forth in a song of ecstatic praise.
- **Future Prophesy 6.** Simeon predicts that the presence of Jesus will be a cause of separation (as at His Trial) between those who denounce Jesus and those who remain faithful to Him.
- **Future Prophesy 7.** Simeon predicts the final moments of Jesus's crucifixion – when a soldier pierces Jesus's side with a sword, to make sure He is actually dead.
- **Coincidence 3.** At the very instant when Simeon completes his prophesy, the old Prophetess Anna appears at the Temple to greet Jesus.
- **Future Prophesy 8.** Anna too predicts that the Baby Jesus will become the world's Redeemer.

Episode 12. The Wise Men

- **Miracle 3.** An unknown Star appears miraculously to astrologers who dwell in the East.
- **Past Prophesy 4.** The Star corresponds to prophesies made in their own Scriptures of a Promised Messiah, or King of the Jews.
- **Past Prophesy 3** (again)**.** The counselors to King Herod interpret the Wise Men's 'King of the Jews' as Micah's prophesy that the Coming Messiah will be born in Bethlehem. (see Episode 8)
- **Miracle 3** (continued)**.** The Star that the Wise Men saw in the East now appears again, this time much closer and moving toward Bethlehem: as if the Star were in fact a bright Angel, or an army of Angels – perhaps the same Angels seen by the Shepherds on the night of Jesus's birth. (see Episode 9)
- **Sign 5.** The Wise Men rejoice at the reappearance of the Star – seeing that as a Sign that their quest for the Messiah is nearing its destination.
- **Future Prophesies 9-11.** The Wise Men present three symbolic gifts – thereby prophesying the Kingship, the Holiness, and the Sacrificial Death of Jesus.
- **Visitation 12.** The Wise Men are warned in a dream of King Herod's evil intentions, and depart without reporting back to him.

Sign 4. The Shepherds find the Baby Jesus wrapped in swaddling clothes lying in a manger.

Episode 13. Flight into Egypt

- **Visitation 13.** Joseph is warned in a dream that King Herod intends to find the promised King of the Jews, and kill him. (see Episode 12)
- **Past Prophesy 5.** Joseph is instructed in his dream to flee into Egypt – in fulfillment of the prediction by the Prophet Hosea over 700 years before, that the Promised Messiah will emerge from that land.

Episode 14. Slaughter of the Innocents

- **Miracle 3 and Past Prophesies 3-4** (referenced). King Herod uses the Miracle of the Star and the Prophesy of Bethlehem to ascertain when and where the promised King of the Jews was born. (see Episodes 8 and 12)
- **Past Prophesy 6.** King Herod slaughters all babies born near Bethlehem within the past two years – in accordance with the prediction made by the Prophet Jeremiah over 600 years before.

Episode 15. Return to Nazareth

- **Visitation 14.** An Angel appears to Joseph in a dream.
- **ESP 4.** The Angel tells Joseph something he could not have known alone -- that King Herod has recently died, and that Joseph can now return safely to Israel. (see Episode 14)
- **Visitation 15.** Joseph Is again visited by the Holy Spirit in a dream – this time encouraging Joseph to return from Egypt, but to shift to a safer destination. (see Episode 14)
- **Past Prophesy 7.** Joseph decides to shift his destination to their original home town in Galilee, Nazareth – in accordance with the unknown prophesy that Jesus will be called a Nazarene. (see Episode 8)

The Whole Story of Christmas

The Whole Story of Christmas: In 16 Episodes

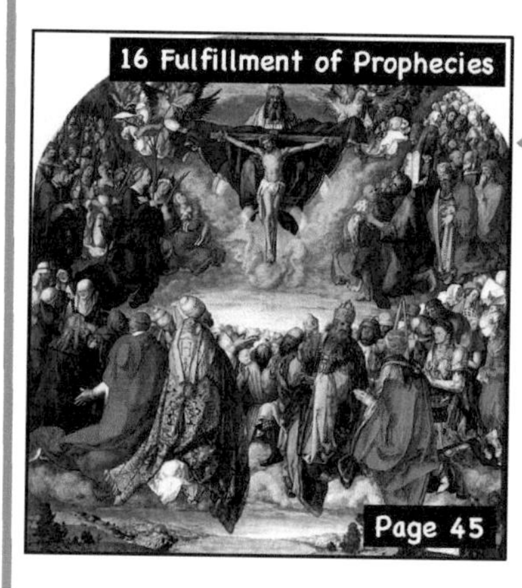

For unto us a child is born, unto us a son is given: and the government shall be upon his shoulder: and his name shall be called Wonderful, Counsellor, The mighty God, The everlasting Father, The Prince of Peace.

Every valley shall be exalted, and every mountain and hill shall be made low: and the crooked shall be made straight, and the rough places plain.

Section A: Before the Birth of Christ

Episode One: Prophesies of the Coming Messiah

Seven hundred years before the Birth of Christ, the Prophet Isaiah bursts forth in praise and thanksgiving for the Coming Messiah. A Messiah who will bring Truth and Justice to the world, and whose birth will be attended by amazing miracles – yet a Messiah who will endure the worst humiliation and suffering as payment for our sins. – Isaiah 7:14; 9:6-7; 40:3-4; 53:3-5.

14 Behold, a virgin shall conceive, and bear a son, and shall call his name Immanuel.

****

6 For unto us a child is born, unto us a son is given: and the government shall be upon his shoulder: and his name shall be called Wonderful, Counsellor, The mighty God, The everlasting Father, The Prince of Peace.

7 Of the increase of his government and peace there shall be no end, upon the throne of David, and upon his kingdom, to order it, and to establish it with judgment and with justice from henceforth even for ever.

****

3 The voice of him that crieth in the wilderness, Prepare ye the way of the Lord, make straight in the desert a highway for our God.

4 Every valley shall be exalted, and every mountain and hill shall be made low: and the crooked shall be made straight, and the rough places plain:

****

3 He is despised and rejected of men; a man of sorrows, and acquainted with grief: and we hid as it were faces from him; he was despised, and we esteemed him not.

4 Surely he hath borne our griefs, and carried our sorrows: yet we did esteem him stricken, smitten of God, and afflicted.

5 But he was wounded for our transgressions, he was bruised for our iniquities: the chastisement of our peace was upon him; and with his stripes we are healed.

Of the increase of his government and peace there shall be no end, upon the throne of David, and upon his kingdom, to order it, and to establish it with judgment and with justice from henceforth even for ever.

GOOD NEWS BIBLE. 14 Well then, the Lord himself will give you a sign: a young woman who is pregnant will have a son and will name him 'Immanuel.' *** 6 A child is born to us! A son is given to us! And he will be our ruler. He will be called, "Wonderful Counselor," "Mighty God," "Eternal Father," "Prince of Peace." 7 His royal power will continue to grow; his kingdom will always be at peace. He will rule as King David's successor, basing his power on right and justice, from now until the end of time. The Lord Almighty is determined to do all this. *** 3 A voice cries out, "Prepare in the wilderness a road for the Lord! Clear the way in the desert for our God! 4 Fill every valley; level every mountain. The hills will become a plain, and the rough country will be made smooth. 5 Then the glory of the Lord will be revealed, and all people will see it. *** 3 We despised him and rejected him; he endured suffering and pain. No one would even look at him - we ignored him as if he were nothing. 4 But he endured the suffering that should have been ours, the pain that we should have borne. All the while we thought that his suffering was punishment sent by God. 5 But because of our sins he was wounded, beaten because of the evil we did. We are healed by the punishment he suffered, made whole by the blows he received.

GOOD NEWS BIBLE. 5 During the time when Herod was king of Judea, there was a priest named Zechariah, who belonged to the
priestly order of Abijah. His wife's name was Elizabeth; she also belonged to a priestly family. 6 They both lived good lives in God's
sight and obeyed fully all the Lord's laws and commands. 7 They had no children because Elizabeth could not have any, and she and
Zechariah were both very old. 8 One day Zechariah was doing his work as a priest in the Temple, taking his turn in the daily service. 9 According to the custom followed by the priests, he was chosen by lot to burn incense on the altar. So he went into the Temple
of the Lord, 10 while the crowd of people outside prayed during the hour when the incense was burned. 11 An angel of the Lord
appeared to him, standing at the right side of the altar where the incense was burned. 12 When Zechariah saw him, he was alarmed
and felt afraid. 13 But the angel said to him, "Don't be afraid, Zechariah! God has heard your prayer, and your wife Elizabeth will bear
you a son. You are to name him John. 14 How glad and happy you will be, and how happy many others will be when he is
born! 15 John will be great in the Lord's sight. He must not drink any wine or strong drink. From his very birth he will be filled with the
Holy Spirit, 16 and he will bring back many of the people of Israel to the Lord their God. 17 He will go ahead of the Lord, strong and
mighty like the prophet Elijah. He will bring fathers and children together again; he will turn disobedient people back to the way of
thinking of the righteous; he will get the Lord's people ready for him." 18 Zechariah said to the angel, "How shall I know if this is so? I
am an old man, and my wife is old also." 19 "I am Gabriel," the angel answered. "I stand in the presence of God, who sent me to speak
to you and tell you this good news. 20 But you have not believed my message, which will come true at the right time. Because you
have not believed, you will be unable to speak; you will remain silent until the day my promise to you comes true." 21 In the meantime
the people were waiting for Zechariah and wondering why he was spending such a long time in the Temple. 22 When he came out,
he could not speak to them, and so they knew that he had seen a vision in the Temple. Unable to say a word, he made signs to them
with his hands. 23 When his period of service in the Temple was over, Zechariah went back home. 24Some time later his wife
Elizabeth became pregnant and did not leave the house for five months. 25 "Now at last the Lord has helped me," she said. "He has
taken away my public disgrace!"

Episode Two:
THE ANNUNCIATION TO ZACHARIAS OF JOHN THE BAPTIST

The Angel Gabriel appears to the old priest Zacharias in the Temple – announcing that his aged and barren wife Elizabeth will give birth to a great holy man named John. This man John will be a Great Reformer – a Prophet who purifies the hearts of the people, so they will be prepared to receive the Coming Messiah. When Zacharias expresses skepticism, because of his wife's advanced age, the Angel strikes him dumb – both as a sign that the Angel's prediction is true, and as a punishment for doubting him. When Zacharias's wife Elizabeth hears of the Prophecy, she too is doubtful – hiding herself from sight, because she fears that pregnancy (and sex!) at her age will make her look ridiculous. – Luke 1:5-25

5 There was in the days of Herod, the king of Judaea, a certain priest named Zacharias, of the course of Abia: and his wife was of the daughters of Aaron, and her name was Elisabeth.

6 And they were both righteous before God, walking in all the commandments and ordinances of the Lord blameless.

7 And they had no child, because that Elisabeth was barren, and they both were well stricken in years.

8 And it came to pass, that while he executed the priest's office before God in the order of his course,

9 According to the custom of the priest's office, his lot was to burn incense when he went into the temple of the Lord.

10 And the whole multitude of the people were praying without at the time of incense.

11 And there appeared unto him an angel of the Lord standing on the right side of the altar of incense.

12 And when Zacharias saw , he was troubled, and fear fell upon him.

13 But the angel said unto him, Fear not, Zacharias: for thy prayer is heard; and thy wife Elisabeth shall bear thee a son, and thou shalt call his name John.

14 And thou shalt have joy and gladness; and many shall rejoice at his birth.

15 For he shall be great in the sight of the Lord, and shall drink neither wine nor strong drink; and he shall be filled with the Holy Ghost, even from his mother's womb.

16 And many of the children of Israel shall he turn to the Lord their God.

17 And he shall go before him in the spirit and power of Elias, to turn the hearts of the fathers to the children, and the disobedient to the wisdom of the just; to make ready a people prepared for the Lord.

18 And Zacharias said unto the angel, Whereby shall I know this? for I am an old man, and my wife well stricken in years.

19 And the angel answering said unto him, I am Gabriel, that stand in the presence of God; and am sent to speak unto thee, and to shew thee these glad tidings.

20 And, behold, thou shalt be dumb, and not able to speak, until the day that these things shall be performed, because thou believest not my words, which shall be fulfilled in their season.

21 And the people waited for Zacharias, and marvelled that he tarried so long in the temple.

22 And when he came out, he could not speak unto them: and they perceived that he had seen a vision in the temple: for he beckoned unto them, and remained speechless.

23 And it came to pass, that, as soon as the days of his ministration were accomplished, he departed to his own house.

24 And after those days his wife Elisabeth conceived, and hid herself five months, saying,

25 Thus hath the Lord dealt with me in the days wherein he looked on me, to take away my reproach among men.

GOOD NEWS BIBLE. 26 In the sixth month of Elizabeth's pregnancy God sent the angel Gabriel to a town in Galilee named Nazareth. 27 He had a message for a young woman promised in marriage to a man named Joseph, who was a descendant of King David. Her name was Mary. 28 The angel came to her and said, "Peace be with you! The Lord is with you and has greatly blessed you!" 29 Mary was deeply troubled by the angel's message, and she wondered what his words meant. 30 The angel said to her, "Don't be afraid, Mary; God has been gracious to you. 31 You will become pregnant and give birth to a son, and you will name him Jesus. 32 He will be great and will be called the Son of the Most High God. The Lord God will make him a king, as his ancestor David was, 33 and he will be the king of the descendants of Jacob forever; his kingdom will never end!" 34 Mary said to the angel, "I am a virgin. How, then, can this be?" 35 The angel answered, "The Holy Spirit will come on you, and God's power will rest upon you. For this reason the holy child will be called the Son of God. 36 Remember your relative Elizabeth. It is said that she cannot have children, but she herself is now six months pregnant, even though she is very old. 37 For there is nothing that God cannot do." 38 "I am the Lord's servant," said Mary; "may it happen to me as you have said." And the angel left her.

Episode Three: The Annunciation to Mary of Jesus Christ

The Angel Gabriel appears to Mary– announcing that she will give birth to Jesus, who will be the Coming Messiah. Mary expresses doubt, because she is a virgin – yet (unlike Zacharias and Elizabeth) when the Angel explains that the Babe will be fathered by the Holy Spirit, Mary humbly accepts the Will of God. As a sign confirming the truth of the Angel's prediction, the Angel discloses that Mary's aged and barren cousin Elizabeth has become pregnant by a Miracle of God. – Luke 1:26-38

26 And in the sixth month the angel Gabriel was sent from God unto a city of Galilee, named Nazareth,

27 To a virgin espoused to a man whose name was Joseph, of the house of David; and the virgin's name Mary.

28 And the angel came in unto her, and said, Hail, thou that art highly favoured, the Lord is with thee: blessed art thou among women.

29 And when she saw him, she was troubled at his saying, and cast in her mind what manner of salutation this should be.

30 And the angel said unto her, Fear not, Mary: for thou hast found favour with God.

31 And, behold, thou shalt conceive in thy womb, and bring forth a son, and shalt call his name Jesus.

32 He shall be great, and shall be called the Son of the Highest: and the Lord God shall give unto him the throne of his father David:

33 And he shall reign over the house of Jacob for ever; and of his kingdom there shall be no end.

34 Then said Mary unto the angel, How shall this be, seeing I know not a man?

35 And the angel answered and said unto her, The Holy Ghost shall come upon thee, and the power of the Highest shall overshadow thee: therefore also that holy thing which shall be born of thee shall be called the Son of God.

36 And, behold, thy cousin Elisabeth, she hath also conceived a son in her old age: and this is the sixth month with her, who was called barren.

37 For with God nothing shall be impossible.

38 And Mary said, Behold the handmaid of the Lord; be it unto me according to thy word. And the angel departed from her.

'Behold the handmaid of the Lord; be it unto me according to thy word.'

And [Elisabeth] spake out with a loud voice, and said, 'Blessed art thou among women, and blessed is the fruit of thy womb.'

Episode Four: The Visit of Mary to Elizabeth

When Mary becomes pregnant with Jesus, she goes to visit her cousin Elizabeth, who (as predicted by the Angel Gabriel) is herself at least six months pregnant. When they meet, the Baby John leaps for joy in Elizabeth's womb, and Elizabeth -- enraptured by the Holy Ghost -- bursts forth with a song of thanksgiving and praise. – Luke 1:39-45

39 And Mary arose in those days, and went into the hill country with haste, into a city of Juda;

40 And entered into the house of Zacharias, and saluted Elisabeth.

41 And it came to pass, that, when Elisabeth heard the salutation of Mary, the babe leaped in her womb; and Elisabeth was filled with the Holy Ghost:

42 And she spake out with a loud voice, and said, Blessed art thou among women, and blessed is the fruit of thy womb.

43 And whence is this to me, that the mother of my Lord should come to me?

44 For, lo, as soon as the voice of thy salutation sounded in mine ears, the babe leaped in my womb for joy.

45 And blessed is she that believed: for there shall be a performance of those things which were told her from the Lord.

When Elisabeth heard the salutation of Mary, the babe leaped in her womb; and Elisabeth was filled with the Holy Ghost.

GOOD NEWS BIBLE. 39 Soon afterward Mary got ready and hurried off to a town in the hill country of Judea. 40 She went into Zechariah's house and greeted Elizabeth. 41 When Elizabeth heard Mary's greeting, the baby moved within her. Elizabeth was filled with the Holy Spirit 42 and said in a loud voice, "You are the most blessed of all women, and blessed is the child you will bear! 43 Why should this great thing happen to me, that my Lord's mother comes to visit me? 44 For as soon as I heard your greeting, the baby within me jumped with gladness. 45 How happy you are to believe that the Lord's message to you will come true!"

'He hath shewed strength with his arm; he hath scattered the proud in the imagination of their hearts. He hath put down the mighty from their seats, and exalted them of low degree.'

Episode Five: The Song of Mary (the Magnificat)

As Mary meets Elizabeth, and hears Elizabeth's song, Mary becomes enraptured by the Holy Spirit. Mary herself bursts forth in a prophetic song – praising God for his immense redemptive power, and thanking God for the Coming Messiah, who will transform the hearts and lives of all humanity. – Luke 1:46-55

46 And Mary said, My soul doth magnify the Lord,

47 And my spirit hath rejoiced in God my Saviour.

48 For he hath regarded the low estate of his handmaiden: for, behold, from henceforth all generations shall call me blessed.

49 For he that is mighty hath done to me great things; and holy is his name.

50 And his mercy is on them that fear him from generation to generation.

51 He hath shewed strength with his arm; he hath scattered the proud in the imagination of their hearts.

52 He hath put down the mighty from their seats, and exalted them of low degree.

53 He hath filled the hungry with good things; and the rich he hath sent empty away.

54 He hath holpen his servant Israel, in remembrance of his mercy;

55 As he spake to our fathers, to Abraham, and to his seed for ever.

'He hath regarded the low estate of his handmaiden: for, behold, from henceforth all generations shall call me blessed.'

GOOD NEWS BIBLE. 46 Mary said, "My heart praises the Lord; 47 my soul is glad because of God my Savior, 48 for he has remembered me, his lowly servant! From now on all people will call me happy, 49 because of the great things the Mighty God has done for me. His name is holy; 50 from one generation to another he shows mercy to those who honor him. 51 He has stretched out his mighty arm and scattered the proud with all their plans. 52 He has brought down mighty kings from their thrones, and lifted up the lowly. 53 He has filled the hungry with good things, and sent the rich away with empty hands. 54 He has kept the promise he made to our ancestors, and has come to the help of his servant Israel. 55 He has remembered to show mercy to Abraham and to all his descendants forever!"

And they made signs to his father, how he would have him called. And he asked for a writing table, and wrote, saying, 'His name is John.' And they marvelled all. And his mouth was opened immediately, and his tongue loosed, and he spake, and praised God.

'And thou, child, shalt be called the prophet of the Highest: for thou shalt go before the face of the Lord to prepare his ways; . . . To give light to them that sit in darkness and in the shadow of death, to guide our feet into the way of peace.'

Episode Six: The Birth of John the Baptist

When Elizabeth's baby is born and brought to the Temple, his father Zacharias surprises the gathered guests by insisting that the baby's name shall be John. At that moment, Zacharias's speech is miraculously restored, and he too is enraptured by the Holy Spirit. Like Mary and Elizabeth, he bursts forth with prophetic utterances – predicting that God will deliver Israel from its present bondage, and that John will be the Prophet who prepares the way for the Coming Messiah. – Luke 1:57-80

57 Now Elisabeth's full time came that she should be delivered; and she brought forth a son.

58 And her neighbours and her cousins heard how the Lord had shewed great mercy upon her; and they rejoiced with her.

59 And it came to pass, that on the eighth day they came to circumcise the child; and they called him Zacharias, after the name of his father.

60 And his mother answered and said, Not ; but he shall be called John.

61 And they said unto her, There is none of thy kindred that is called by this name.

62 And they made signs to his father, how he would have him called.

63 And he asked for a writing table, and wrote, saying, His name is John. And they marvelled all.

64 And his mouth was opened immediately, and his tongue loosed, and he spake, and praised God.

65 And fear came on all that dwelt round about them: and all these sayings were noised abroad throughout all the hill country of Judaea.

66 And all they that heard them laid them up in their hearts, saying, What manner of child shall this be! And the hand of the Lord was with him.

67 And his father Zacharias was filled with the Holy Ghost, and prophesied, saying,

68 Blessed the Lord God of Israel; for he hath visited and redeemed his people,

69 And hath raised up an horn of salvation for us in the house of his servant David;

70 As he spake by the mouth of his holy prophets, which have been since the world began:

71 That we should be saved from our enemies, and from the hand of all that hate us;

72 To perform the mercy promised to our fathers, and to remember his holy covenant;

73 The oath which he sware to our father Abraham,

74 That he would grant unto us, that we being delivered out of the hand of our enemies might serve him without fear,

75 In holiness and righteousness before him, all the days of our life.

76 And thou, child, shalt be called the prophet of the Highest: for thou shalt go before the face of the Lord to prepare his ways;

77 To give knowledge of salvation unto his people by the remission of their sins,

78 Through the tender mercy of our God; whereby the dayspring from on high hath visited us,

79 To give light to them that sit in darkness and in the shadow of death, to guide our feet into the way of peace.

80 And the child grew, and waxed strong in spirit, and was in the deserts till the day of his shewing unto Israel.

GOOD NEWS BIBLE. 57 The time came for Elizabeth to have her baby, and she gave birth to a son. 58 Her neighbors and relatives heard how wonderfully good the Lord had been to her, and they all rejoiced with her. 59 When the baby was a week old, they came to circumcise him, and they were going to name him Zechariah, after his father. 60 But his mother said, "No! His name is to be John." 61 They said to her, "But you don't have any relative with that name!" 62 Then they made signs to his father, asking him what name he would like the boy to have. 63 Zechariah asked for a writing pad and wrote, "His name is John." How surprised they all were! 64 At that moment Zechariah was able to speak again, and he started praising God. 65 The neighbors were all filled with fear, and the news about these things spread through all the hill country of Judea. 66 Everyone who heard of it thought about it and asked, "What is this child going to be?" For it was plain that the Lord's power was upon him. 67 John's father Zechariah was filled with the Holy Spirit, and he spoke God's message: 68 "Let us praise the Lord, the God of Israel! He has come to the help of his people and has set them free. 69 He has provided for us a mighty Savior, a descendant of his servant David. 70 He promised through his holy prophets long ago 71 that he would save us from our enemies, from the power of all those who hate us. 72 He said he would show mercy to our ancestors and remember his sacred covenant. 73 With a solemn oath to our ancestor Abraham he promised to rescue us from our enemies and allow us to serve him without fear, 75 so that we might be holy and righteous before him all the days of our life. 76 "You, my child, will be called a prophet of the Most High God. You will go ahead of the Lord to prepare his road for him, 77 to tell his people that they will be saved by having their sins forgiven. 78 Our God is merciful and tender. He will cause the bright dawn of salvation to rise on us 79 and to shine from heaven on all those who live in the dark shadow of death, to guide our steps into the path of peace." 80 The child grew and developed in body and spirit. He lived in the desert until the day when he appeared publicly to the people of Israel.

Behold, the angel of the Lord appeared unto him in a dream, saying, 'Joseph, thou son of David, fear not to take unto thee Mary thy wife: for that which is conceived in her is of the Holy Ghost.'
'Behold, a virgin shall be with child, and shall bring forth a son, and they shall call his name Emmanuel, which being interpreted is, God with us.'

SECTION B: THE BIRTH OF CHRIST

Episode Seven: The Annunciation to Joseph of the Coming Messiah

Before Joseph and Mary are intimate, Mary discloses that she has become pregnant. Believing Mary to have been unfaithful, yet not wishing to condemn her to punishment, Joseph decides to end their betrothal quietly. But in a dream, an angel explains to Joseph that Mary's future child is not the result of fornication -- but has been fathered by the Holy Spirit, as predicted by the Prophet Isaiah. In obedience to God's Will, Joseph decides to continue with their marriage plans, and to abstain from sex until after their miracle child is born. – Matthew 1:18-25

18 Now the birth of Jesus Christ was on this wise: When as his mother Mary was espoused to Joseph, before they came together, she was found with child of the Holy Ghost.

19 Then Joseph her husband, being a just man, and not willing to make her a publick example, was minded to put her away privily.

20 But while he thought on these things, behold, the angel of the Lord appeared unto him in a dream, saying, Joseph, thou son of David, fear not to take unto thee Mary thy wife: for that which is conceived in her is of the Holy Ghost.

21 And she shall bring forth a son, and thou shalt call his name Jesus: for he shall save his people from their sins.

22 Now all this was done, that it might be fulfilled which was spoken of the Lord by the prophet, saying,

23 Behold, a virgin shall be with child, and shall bring forth a son, and they shall call his name Emmanuel, which being interpreted is, God with us.

24 Then Joseph being raised from sleep did as the angel of the Lord had bidden him, and took unto him his wife:

25 And knew her not till she had brought forth her firstborn son: and he called his name Jesus.

Then Joseph being raised from sleep did as the angel of the Lord had bidden him, and took unto him his wife: And knew her not till she had brought forth her firstborn son.

GOOD NEWS BIBLE. 18 This was how the birth of Jesus Christ took place. His mother Mary was engaged to Joseph, but before they were married, she found out that she was going to have a baby by the Holy Spirit. 19 Joseph was a man who always did what was right, but he did not want to disgrace Mary publicly; so he made plans to break the engagement privately. 20 While he was thinking about this, an angel of the Lord appeared to him in a dream and said, "Joseph, descendant of David, do not be afraid to take Mary to be your wife. For it is by the Holy Spirit that she has conceived. 21 She will have a son, and you will name him Jesus - because he will save his people from their sins." 22 Now all this happened in order to make come true what the Lord had said through the prophet, 23 "A virgin will become pregnant and have a son, and he will be called Immanuel" (which means, "God is with us"). 24 So when Joseph woke up, he married Mary, as the angel of the Lord had told him to. 25 But he had no sexual relations with her before she gave birth to her son. And Joseph named him Jesus.

There went out a decree from Caesar Augustus, that all the world should be taxed.
And Joseph also went up from Galilee, out of the city of Nazareth, into Judaea, unto the city of David, which is called Bethlehem; (because he was of the house and lineage of David:) To be taxed with Mary his espoused wife, being great with child.

Episode Eight: The Journey of Joseph and Mary to Bethlehem

The Emperor Augustus in Rome decides to raise money by taxing everyone in his empire – which requires every citizen to return to his home town to be accounted for. Thus, Joseph travels from Nazareth to his ancestral home village of Bethlehem -- bringing his betrothed and pregnant wife Mary, and residing there until their child is born. – Luke 2:1-6

1 And it came to pass in those days, that there went out a decree from Caesar Augustus, that all the world should be taxed.

2 (And this taxing was first made when Cyrenius was governor of Syria.)

3 And all went to be taxed, every one into his own city.

4 And Joseph also went up from Galilee, out of the city of Nazareth, into Judaea, unto the city of David, which is called Bethlehem; (because he was of the house and lineage of David:)

5 To be taxed with Mary his espoused wife, being great with child.

6 And so it was, that, while they were there, the days were accomplished that she should be delivered.

GOOD NEWS BIBLE. 1 At that time Emperor Augustus ordered a census to be taken throughout the Roman Empire. 2 When this first census took place, Quirinius was the governor of Syria. 3 Everyone, then, went to register himself, each to his own hometown. 4 Joseph went from the town of Nazareth in Galilee to the town of Bethlehem in Judea, the birthplace of King David. Joseph went there because he was a descendant of David. 5 He went to register with Mary, who was promised in marriage to him. She was pregnant, 6 and while they were in Bethlehem, the time came for her to have her baby.

And, lo, the angel of the Lord came upon them, and the glory of the Lord shone round about them: and they were sore afraid.
And the angel said unto them, 'Fear not: for, behold, I bring you good tidings of great joy, which shall be to all people. For unto you is born this day in the city of David a Saviour, which is Christ the Lord.'

Episode Nine: The Annunciation to the Shepherds

While a group of shepherds are out tending their flock at night, an Angel comes hovering with blinding brightness above them. He quiets their fears, and announces the Good News -- the birth of a Holy Savior in nearby Bethlehem. As proof, the Angel predicts that the shepherds will find the Babe lying in a manger in a humble stable. With that, there appears above the shepherds a great army of angels – praising God and glorifying His great gift to mankind.
– Luke 2:8-14

8 And there were in the same country shepherds abiding in the field, keeping watch over their flock by night.

9 And, lo, the angel of the Lord came upon them, and the glory of the Lord shone round about them: and they were sore afraid.

10 And the angel said unto them, Fear not: for, behold, I bring you good tidings of great joy, which shall be to all people.

11 For unto you is born this day in the city of David a Saviour, which is Christ the Lord.

12 And this shall be a sign unto you; Ye shall find the babe wrapped in swaddling clothes, lying in a manger.

13 And suddenly there was with the angel a multitude of the heavenly host praising God, and saying,

14 Glory to God in the highest, and on earth peace, good will toward men.

GOOD NEWS BIBLE. 8 There were some shepherds in that part of the country who were spending the night in the fields, taking care of their flocks. 9 An angel of the Lord appeared to them, and the glory of the Lord shone over them. They were terribly afraid, 10 but the angel said to them, "Don't be afraid! I am here with good news for you, which will bring great joy to all the people. 11 This very day in David's town your Savior was born - Christ the Lord! 12 And this is what will prove it to you: you will find a baby wrapped in cloths and lying in a manger." 13 Suddenly a great army of heaven's angels appeared with the angel, singing praises to God: 14 "Glory to God in the highest heaven, and peace on earth to those with whom he is pleased!"

And it came to pass, as the angels were gone away from them into heaven, the shepherds said one to another, 'Let us now go even unto Bethlehem, and see this thing which is come to pass, which the Lord hath made known unto us.'

And when [the shepherds] had seen it, they made known abroad the saying which was told them concerning this child. And all they that heard it wondered at those things which were told them by the shepherds.

Episode Ten: The Nativity of Jesus Christ at the Manger

When Joseph and Mary arrive in Bethlehem, they find refuge in a stable – because all the inns are full, as a result of the census. When the Baby Jesus is born shortly thereafter, they wrap Him in swaddling clothes, and lay Him in the only cradle available – a manger, or eating-trough for cattle. That very night, the shepherds from the hillside arrive and gather around the manger -- worshipping the Babe in joy and amazement, then spreading the wonderful news to the surrounding countryside. Meanwhile, Mary continues to be perplexed – wondering how she should be chosen for such a central role in this miraculous event. – Luke 2:7, 15-20

7 And [Mary] brought forth her firstborn son, and wrapped him in swaddling clothes, and laid him in a manger; because there was no room for them in the inn...

15 And it came to pass, as the angels were gone away from them into heaven, the shepherds said one to another, Let us now go even unto Bethlehem, and see this thing which is come to pass, which the Lord hath made known unto us.

16 And they came with haste, and found Mary, and Joseph, and the babe lying in a manger.

17 And when they had seen it, they made known abroad the saying which was told them concerning this child.

18 And all they that heard it wondered at those things which were told them by the shepherds.

19 But Mary kept all these things, and pondered them in her heart.

20 And the shepherds returned, glorifying and praising God for all the things that they had heard and seen, as it was told unto them.

And they came with haste, and found Mary, and Joseph, and the babe lying in a manger.

GOOD NEWS BIBLE. 7 She gave birth to her first son, wrapped him in cloths and laid him in a manger - there was no room for them to stay in the inn. ... 15 When the angels went away from them back into heaven, the shepherds said to one another, "Let's go to Bethlehem and see this thing that has happened, which the Lord has told us." 16 So they hurried off and found Mary and Joseph and saw the baby lying in the manger. 17 When the shepherds saw him, they told them what the angel had said about the child. 18 All who heard it were amazed at what the shepherds said. 19 Mary remembered all these things and thought deeply about them. 20 The shepherds went back, singing praises to God for all they had heard and seen; it had been just as the angel had told them.

GOOD NEWS BIBLE. 21 A week later, when the time came for the baby to be circumcised, he was named Jesus, the name which the angel had given him before he had been conceived. 22 The time came for Joseph and Mary to perform the ceremony of purification, as the Law of Moses commanded. So they took the child to Jerusalem to present him to the Lord, 23 as it is written in the law of the Lord: "Every first-born male is to be dedicated to the Lord." 24 They also went to offer a sacrifice of a pair of doves or two young pigeons, as required by the law of the Lord. 25 At that time there was a man named Simeon living in Jerusalem. He was a good, God-fearing man and was waiting for Israel to be saved. The Holy Spirit was with him 26 and had assured him that he would not die before he had seen the Lord's promised Messiah. 27 Led by the Spirit, Simeon went into the Temple. When the parents brought the child Jesus into the Temple to do for him what the Law required, 28 Simeon took the child in his arms and gave thanks to God: 29 "Now, Lord, you have kept your promise, and you may let your servant go in peace. 30 With my own eyes I have seen your salvation, 31 which you have prepared in the presence of all peoples: 32 A light to reveal your will to the Gentiles and bring glory to your people Israel." 33 The child's father and mother were amazed at the things Simeon said about him. 34 Simeon blessed them and said to Mary, his mother, "This child is chosen by God for the destruction and the salvation of many in Israel. He will be a sign from God which many people will speak against 35 and so reveal their secret thoughts. And sorrow, like a sharp sword, will break your own heart." 36 There was a very old prophet, a widow named Anna, daughter of Phanuel of the tribe of Asher. She had been married for only seven years and was now eighty-four years old. She never left the Temple; day and night she worshiped God, fasting and praying. 38 That very same hour she arrived and gave thanks to God and spoke about the child to all who were waiting for God to set Jerusalem free.

Section C: After the Birth of Christ

Episode Eleven: The Presentation at the Temple with Simeon and Anna

A week after the birth, Joseph and Mary bring Jesus to the temple to be circumcised. Then, forty days after the birth, they bring Jesus again to the temple for the traditional presentation and ritual sacrifice. There, they encounter an old man named Simeon -- who has been long awaiting the coming Messiah, and who has been impelled by the Holy Spirit at that very moment to appear and greet the Promised One. Simeon bursts into a song of praise and thanksgiving for the now-arrived Messiah – a Prophet who will exalt the righteous, yet reveal the base hearts of those who reject him. At that very moment, an ancient prophetess named Anna also appears – recognizing Jesus as the Promised Redeemer and praising God for His coming.

– Luke 2:21-38

21 And when eight days were accomplished for the circumcising of the child, his name was called Jesus, which was so named of the angel before he was conceived in the womb.

22 And when the days of her purification according to the law of Moses were accomplished, they brought him to Jerusalem, to present to the Lord;

23 (As it is written in the law of the Lord, Every male that openeth the womb shall be called holy to the Lord;)

24 And to offer a sacrifice according to that which is said in the law of the Lord, A pair of turtledoves, or two young pigeons.

25 And, behold, there was a man in Jerusalem, whose name was Simeon; and the same man was just and devout, waiting for the consolation of Israel: and the Holy Ghost was upon him.

26 And it was revealed unto him by the Holy Ghost, that he should not see death, before he had seen the Lord's Christ.

27 And he came by the Spirit into the temple: and when the parents brought in the child Jesus, to do for him after the custom of the law,

28 Then took he him up in his arms, and blessed God, and said,

29 Lord, now lettest thou thy servant depart in peace, according to thy word:

30 For mine eyes have seen thy salvation,

31 Which thou hast prepared before the face of all people;

32 A light to lighten the Gentiles, and the glory of thy people Israel.

33 And Joseph and his mother marvelled at those things which were spoken of him.

34 And Simeon blessed them, and said unto Mary his mother, Behold, this child is set for the fall and rising again of many in Israel; and for a sign which shall be spoken against;

35 (Yea, a sword shall pierce through thy own soul also,) that the thoughts of many hearts may be revealed.

36 And there was one Anna, a prophetess, the daughter of Phanuel, of the tribe of Aser: she was of a great age, and had lived with an husband seven years from her virginity;

37 And she was a widow of about fourscore and four years, which departed not from the temple, but served God with fastings and prayers night and day.

38 And she coming in that instant gave thanks likewise unto the Lord, and spake of him to all them that looked for redemption in Jerusalem.

And [Anna] coming in that instant gave thanks likewise unto the Lord, and spake of him to all them that looked for redemption in Jerusalem.

GOOD NEWS BIBLE. 1 Jesus was born in the town of Bethlehem in Judea, during the
time when Herod was king. Soon afterward, some men who studied the stars came
from the East to Jerusalem 2 and asked, "Where is the baby born to be the king of
the Jews? We saw his star when it came up in the east, and we have come to worship
him." 3 When King Herod heard about this, he was very upset, and so was everyone
else in Jerusalem. 4 He called together all the chief priests and the teachers of the
Law and asked them, "Where will the Messiah be born?" 5"In the town of Bethlehem
in Judea," they answered. "For this is what the prophet wrote: 6"Bethlehem in the
land of Judah, you are by no means the least of the leading cities of Judah; for from
you will come a leader who will guide my people Israel.' " 7 So Herod called the visitors from the East to a secret meeting and found out from them the exact time the star
had appeared. 8 Then he sent them to Bethlehem with these instructions: "Go and
make a careful search for the child; and when you find him, let me know, so that I too
may go and worship him." 9 And so they left, and on their way they saw the same
star they had seen in the East. When they saw it, how happy they were, what joy was
theirs! It went ahead of them until it stopped over the place where the child
was. 11 They went into the house, and when they saw the child with his mother Mary,
they knelt down and worshiped him. They brought out their gifts of gold, frankincense,
and myrrh, and presented them to him. 12 Then they returned to their country by another road, since God had warned them in a dream not to go back to Herod.

Episode Twelve: The Visit of the Wise Men (the Magi)

When Jesus is a little child, three Wise Men from the East ('Magi') appear in Jerusalem – asking where they might find the prophesied Messiah. Almost two years ago, these Magi saw the 'star' of Jesus's birth (perhaps actually the same army of angels seen by the shepherds, Episode 9) – and they have been travelling ever since from their distant land. On the advice of his scriptural counselors, Herod directs the Magi to the little town of Bethlehem – where this 'King of the Jews' supposedly will be born. Fearing a threat to his rule, King Herod instructs the Magi to report back to him – so he can take action (Episode 14), once they have verified that the Child is in fact the Messiah. A star much like the one the Magi first saw in the East now guides them straight to Jesus. When they find the young Christ (no longer in the manger, of course), they bend down and worship Him – offering gifts that symbolize His kingship, His holiness, and His sacrificial death. Then, being warned in a dream that Herod has evil intentions, the Wise Men depart without reporting back to Herod what they have found. – Luke 2:21-38

1 Now when Jesus was born in Bethlehem of Judaea in the days of Herod the king, behold, there came wise men from the east to Jerusalem,

2 Saying, Where is he that is born King of the Jews? for we have seen his star in the east, and are come to worship him.

3 When Herod the king had heard these , he was troubled, and all Jerusalem with him.

4 And when he had gathered all the chief priests and scribes of the people together, he demanded of them where Christ should be born.

5 And they said unto him, In Bethlehem of Judaea: for thus it is written by the prophet,

6 And thou Bethlehem, in the land of Juda, art not the least among the princes of Juda: for out of thee shall come a Governor, that shall rule my people Israel.

7 Then Herod, when he had privily called the wise men, enquired of them diligently what time the star appeared.

8 And he sent them to Bethlehem, and said, Go and search diligently for the young child; and when ye have found him, bring me word again, that I may come and worship him also.

9 When they had heard the king, they departed; and, lo, the star, which they saw in the east, went before them, till it came and stood over where the young child was.

10 When they saw the star, they rejoiced with exceeding great joy.

11 And when they were come into the house, they saw the young child with Mary his mother, and fell down, and worshipped him: and when they had opened their treasures, they presented unto him gifts; gold, and frankincense, and myrrh.

12 And being warned of God in a dream that they should not return to Herod, they departed into their own country another way.

And when they were come into the house, they saw the young child with Mary his mother, and fell down, and worshipped him: and when they had opened their treasures, they presented unto him gifts; gold, and frankincense, and myrrh.

Behold, the angel of the Lord appeareth to Joseph in a dream, saying, 'Arise, and take the young child and his mother, and flee into Egypt.'

When [Joseph] arose, he took the young child and his mother by night, and departed into Egypt.

Episode Thirteen: The Flight into Egypt

After the Wise Men leave, Joseph is warned in a dream that King Herod intends to kill their baby – because he views this coming 'King of the Jews' as a threat to his rule. That night, Joseph and Mary depart in haste for Egypt. – Matthew 2:13-15

13 And when [the Wise Men] were departed, behold, the angel of the Lord appeareth to Joseph in a dream, saying, Arise, and take the young child and his mother, and flee into Egypt, and be thou there until I bring thee word: for Herod will seek the young child to destroy him.

14 When he arose, he took the young child and his mother by night, and departed into Egypt:

15 And was there until the death of Herod: that it might be fulfilled which was spoken of the Lord by the prophet, saying, Out of Egypt have I called my son.

GOOD NEWS BIBLE. 13 After they had left, an angel of the Lord appeared in a dream to Joseph and said, "Herod will be looking for the child in order to kill him. So get up, take the child and his mother and escape to Egypt, and stay there until I tell you to leave." 14 Joseph got up, took the child and his mother, and left during the night for Egypt, 15 where he stayed until Herod died. This was done to make come true what the Lord had said through the prophet, "I called my Son out of Egypt."

Then Herod, when he saw that he was mocked of the wise men, was exceeding wroth, and sent forth, and slew all the children that were in Bethlehem, and in all the coasts thereof, from two years old and under...
In Rama was there a voice heard, lamentation, and weeping, and great mourning, Rachel weeping for her children, and would not be comforted, because they are not.

Episode Fourteen: The Slaughter of the Innocents

The fearful and paranoid King Herod is enraged that the Wise Men have departed without reporting back to him. Not knowing which recently-born baby is the coming 'King of the Jews,' Herod orders all the male children born near Bethlehem within the last two years to be slaughtered – an event predicted by the Prophet Jeremiah over 600 years before. – Matthew 2:16-18

16 Then Herod, when he saw that he was mocked of the wise men, was exceeding wroth, and sent forth, and slew all the children that were in Bethlehem, and in all the coasts thereof, from two years old and under, according to the time which he had diligently enquired of the wise men.

17 Then was fulfilled that which was spoken by Jeremy the prophet, saying,

18 In Rama was there a voice heard, lamentation, and weeping, and great mourning, Rachel weeping for her children, and would not be comforted, because they are not.

GOOD NEWS BIBLE. 16 When Herod realized that the visitors from the East had tricked him, he was furious. He gave orders to kill all the boys in Bethlehem and its neighborhood who were two years old and younger - this was done in accordance with what he had learned from the visitors about the time when the star had appeared. 17 In this way what the prophet Jeremiah had said came true: 18 "A sound is heard in Ramah, the sound of bitter weeping. Rachel is crying for her children; she refuses to be comforted, for they are dead."

'Arise, and take the young child and his mother, and go into the land of Israel: for they are dead which sought the young child's life.'
Being warned of God in a dream, he turned aside into the parts of Galilee: And he came and dwelt in a city called Nazareth: that it might be fulfilled which was spoken by the prophets, 'He shall be called a Nazarene.'

Episode Fifteen: The Return of Joseph and Mary to Nazareth

After a few years, Joseph receives another dream – informing him that the vengeful King Herod is now dead, and that they can now safely return to Israel. However, upon learning that Herod's son Archelaus is now ruler, Joseph decides it is more prudent to settle, not in Judea, but in their original home town of Nazareth in Galilee. There, Jesus grows to be a strong and wise young boy, filled with the Grace of God. – Matthew 2:19-23; Luke 2:40.

19 But when Herod was dead, behold, an angel of the Lord appeareth in a dream to Joseph in Egypt,

20 Saying, Arise, and take the young child and his mother, and go into the land of Israel: for they are dead which sought the young child's life.

21 And he arose, and took the young child and his mother, and came into the land of Israel.

22 But when he heard that Archelaus did reign in Judaea in the room of his father Herod, he was afraid to go thither: notwithstanding, being warned of God in a dream, he turned aside into the parts of Galilee:

23 And he came and dwelt in a city called Nazareth: that it might be fulfilled which was spoken by the prophets, He shall be called a Nazarene.

****

40 And the child grew, and waxed strong in spirit, filled with wisdom: and the grace of God was upon him.

And the child grew, and waxed strong in spirit, filled with wisdom: and the grace of God was upon him.

GOOD NEWS BIBLE. (Matthew 2) 19 After Herod died, an angel of the Lord appeared in a dream to Joseph in Egypt
20 and said, "Get up, take the child and his mother, and go back to the land of Israel, because those who tried to kill
the child are dead." 21 So Joseph got up, took the child and his mother, and went back to Israel. 22 But when Joseph heard that Archelaus had succeeded his father Herod as king of Judea, he was afraid to go there. He was
given more instructions in a dream, so he went to the province of Galilee 23 and made his home in a town named
Nazareth. And so what the prophets had said came true: "He will be called a Nazarene." *** (Luke 2) 40 The child
grew and became strong; he was full of wisdom, and God's blessings were upon him.

And they sung a new song, saying, 'Thou art worthy to take the book, and to open the seals thereof: for thou wast slain, and hast redeemed us to God by thy blood out of every kindred, and tongue, and people, and nation.'

A great multitude, which no man could number, of all nations, and kindreds, and people, and tongues, stood before the throne, and before the Lamb, clothed with white robes, and palms in their hands.

GOOD NEWS BIBLE. (Matt 28.) 18 Jesus drew near and said to them, "I have been given all authority in heaven and on
earth. 19 Go, then, to all peoples everywhere and make them my disciples: baptize them in the name of the Father,
the Son, and the Holy Spirit, 20 and teach them to obey everything I have commanded you. And I will be with you
always, to the end of the age."*** (Rev 5.) 7 The Lamb went and took the scroll from the right hand of the one who
sits on the throne. 8 As he did so, the four living creatures and the twenty-four elders fell down before the Lamb.
Each had a harp and gold bowls filled with incense, which are the prayers of God's people. 9 They sang a new
song: "You are worthy to take the scroll and to break open its seals. For you were killed, and by your sacrificial death
you bought for God people from every tribe, language, nation, and race. 10 You have made them a kingdom of
priests to serve our God, and they shall rule on earth." *** (Rev 7.) 9 After this I looked, and there was an enormous
crowd - no one could count all the people! They were from every race, tribe, nation, and language, and they stood in
front of the throne and of the Lamb, dressed in white robes and holding palm branches in their hands. 10 They called
out in a loud voice: "Salvation comes from our God, who sits on the throne, and from the Lamb!"

Episode 16: The Fulfillment of the Prophecies

Toward the end of Jesus's life, and after his death, there are further prophecies – many of these fulfilling the prophecies made before Jesus's birth. At the end of the Gospels, Jesus tells us that that Good News of Christ's Salvation will be spread to the far ends of the Earth. In the Book of Revelation, we find that the Lamb of Christ will be acknowledged as Lord and Savior by all peoples, all languages, all cultures, all nations.
– Matthew 28:18-20; Revelation 5:7-9. 7:9-10.

18 And Jesus came and spake unto them, saying, All power is given unto me in heaven and in earth.

19 Go ye therefore, and teach all nations, baptizing them in the name of the Father, and of the Son, and of the Holy Ghost:

20 Teaching them to observe all things whatsoever I have commanded you: and, lo, I am with you alway, even unto the end of the world.

***

7 And [the Lamb] came and took the book out of the right hand of him that sat upon the throne.

8 And when he had taken the book, the four beasts and four and twenty elders fell down before the Lamb, having every one of them harps, and golden vials full of odours, which are the prayers of saints.

9 And they sung a new song, saying, Thou art worthy to take the book, and to open the seals thereof: for thou wast slain, and hast redeemed us to God by thy blood out of every kindred, and tongue, and people, and nation;

10 And hast made us unto our God kings and priests: and we shall reign on the earth.

***

9 After this I beheld, and, lo, a great multitude, which no man could number, of all nations, and kindreds, and people, and tongues, stood before the throne, and before the Lamb, clothed with white robes, and palms in their hands;

10 And cried with a loud voice, saying, Salvation to our God which sitteth upon the throne, and unto the Lamb.

Made in the USA
Columbia, SC
10 December 2024